US Citizenship Test Study Guide

2021 & 2022

Naturalization Test Prep for all
100 USCIS Civics Questions and
Answers [3rd Edition]

Greg Bridges

Table of Contents

Introduction

Function of the Test

The naturalization test is for non-U.S. citizens who are hoping to become U.S. citizens. The naturalization test is given during the U.S. citizenship interview. After the U.S. citizenship interview is passed, you will take an Oath of Allegiance at a naturalization ceremony.

According to the U.S. Citizenship and Immigration Services, 91 percent of those who take the test end up passing it.

Test Administration and Format

Those who wish to become U.S. citizens must first apply for naturalization and make sure they meet the requirements. Then the naturalization test will be given at the naturalization interview.

During the naturalization interview, a USCIS officer will ask questions about your background and application. You will then take an English test and a civics test. This guide is only for the civics test. We have provided the 100 possible test questions. You will be asked 10 of these 100 questions during the test. You will have to answer 6 out of 10 questions correctly to pass it.

The civics exam tests you on U.S. history and government knowledge. The questions will be asked to you by a USCIS officer. Then, you will say the answers out loud.

Anyone who fails the naturalization exam will be given a second opportunity to pass. After a second failed attempt, you may reapply for naturalization, or you may appeal the decision.

Exam Tips

Sometimes a question has multiple correct answers. For example:

2. What does the Constitution do?

- Sets up the government
- Defines the government
- Protects the basic rights of Americans

For this question, all three answers listed are correct. You must only say one of those answers.

Other questions also have multiple correct answers and require you to give multiple answers:

9. What are two rights in the Declaration of Independence?

- Life
- Liberty
- Pursuit of happiness

In this case, all three answers are correct, but you must say two of the answers.

Be sure to read the questions carefully to know how many answers you need to memorize.

Note

* If you are 65 years old or older and have been a legal permanent resident of the United States for 20 or more years, you may study just the questions that have been marked with an asterisk. You will only be asked questions from that set of 20 questions.

American Government

Principles of American Democracy

1. What is the supreme law of the land?

- The Constitution

The highest law is the Constitution. The government cannot pass a law that goes against the Constitution. The Supreme Court can say that state or federal laws are unlawful if a new law goes against the constitution.

2. What does the Constitution do?

- Sets up the government
- Defines the government
- Protects the basic rights of Americans

The Constitution sets up a national government made of three branches: legislative, executive, and judicial. The Constitution also divides federal and state power. Finally, the constitution protects the freedoms of citizens outlined in the Bill of Rights.

3. The idea of self-government is in the first three words of the Constitution. What are these words?

- We the People

The first sentence of the Constitution (called the Preamble) is this: "We the People of the United States, in order to form a more perfect union, establish justice, insure domestic tranquility, provide for the common defense, promote the general welfare, and secure the blessing of liberty to ourselves and our posterity, do ordain and establish this Constitution for the United States of America." The preamble explains why the Constitution was written.

4. What is an amendment?

- A change to the Constitution
- An addition to the Constitution

Amendments are the only way to change the Constitution. To become a usable part of the Constitution, an amendment must be approved by three-fourths of the legislatures or state ratifying conventions. After the Archivist's consent, the amendment can move forward as part of the Constitution.

5. What do we call the first ten amendments to the Constitution?

- The Bill of Rights

The Bill of Rights was approved in 1791. It pledges personal rights and freedoms. It limits government power. It also says that powers not delegated to Congress should be reserved for the states or the people.

6. What is one right or freedom from the First Amendment?*

- Speech
- Religion
- Assembly
- Press
- Petition the government

The first amendment is this: "Congress shall make no law respecting an establishment of religion, or prohibiting the free exercise thereof; or abridging the freedom of speech, or of the press; or the right of the people peaceably to assemble, and to petition the Government for a redress of grievances."

7. How many amendments does the Constitution have?

- Twenty-seven (27)

The Constitution has 27 amendments. The first ten amendments were adopted at the same time. These are called the Bill of Rights. It is not ideal for the Constitution to constantly change. This is why amendments must be proposed and approved before going into effect.

8. What did the Declaration of Independence do?

- Announced our independence from Great Britain
- Declared our Independence from Great Britain
- Said that the United States is free from Great Britain

The Declaration of Independence is a written statement. It announced independence from Great Britain. It declared that the colonies were thirteen independent states. The Declaration of Independence was approved on July 4, 1776.

9. What are two rights in the Declaration of Independence?

- Life
- Liberty
- Pursuit of happiness

There are three unalienable Rights mentioned in the Constitution. These are life, liberty, and the pursuit of happiness. The phrase is taken from this sentence: "We hold these truths to be self-evident, that all men are created equal, that they are endowed by their Creator with certain unalienable Rights, that among these are Life, Liberty and the pursuit of Happiness."

10. What is freedom of religion?

- You can practice any religion, or not practice a religion.

Freedom of religion is outlined in the First Amendment. It says that Congress cannot make a law regarding an establishment of religion. It also says that Congress cannot make a law banning a religion from being practiced.

11. What is the economic system in the United States?*

- Capitalist economy
- Market economy

The economic system in the United States is a market economy. This means that the U.S. has individual producers and consumers who decide on goods and services. They also decide their own prices. Government plays a limited role in the U.S. market economy. However, it does provide assistance programs, national defense, and interstate highways and airports.

12. What is the "rule of law"?

- Everyone must follow the law.
- Leaders must obey the law.
- Government must obey the law.
- No one is above the law.

"Rule of law" is how a country's laws influence the society and its people. The rule of law is an ideal where everyone is treated equally before the law. Someone's rank or wealth does not come into consideration under the rule of law. Everyone is treated the same.

System of Government

13. Name one branch or part of the government.*

- Congress
- Legislative
- President
- Executive
- The courts
- Judicial

The three branches of government are legislative, executive, and judicial. The president is part of the executive branch. Congress makes up the legislative branch. The courts (Supreme Court and lower courts) make up the judicial branch.

14. What stops one branch of government from becoming too powerful?

- Checks and balances
- Separation of powers

Separation of powers is when the government is divided into separate branches. It keeps one branch from becoming too powerful. In the U.S., the judicial, legislative, and executive branches are separated. They have the power to "check" each other to make sure the balance is equal. The power of these branches to check one another is called "checks and balances."

15. Who is in charge of the executive branch?

- The president

The president is head of the executive branch. The executive branch is set up to enforce and execute the law. The president also acts as Commander-in-Chief of the military.

16. Who makes federal laws?

- Congress
- Senate and House of Representatives
- U.S. or national legislature

The branch that writes the laws is known as the legislative branch. This branch is made up of two chambers: the Senate and the House of Representatives, also known as Congress. The U.S. legislature, Congress, or Senate and House of Representatives are all appropriate answers.

17. What are the two parts of the U.S. Congress?*

- The Senate and the House of Representatives

The Senate and House of Representatives make up Congress. This part of the government is considered the bicameral legislative branch. It creates and writes the laws.

18. How many U.S. Senators are there?

- One hundred (100)

There are 2 Senators chosen to represent each state. There are 50 states. Thus, there are 100 Senators.

19. We elect a U.S. Senator for how many years?

- Six (6)

U.S. Senators remain in office for 6 years. One-third of the Senate membership is elected every two years.

20. Who is one of your state's U.S. Senators now?*

- Answers will vary according to your state. You can find your U.S. Senators here: whoismyrepresenative.com

  Those who live in the District of Columbia or U.S. territories should answer that these places have zero U.S. Senators.

21. The House of Representatives has how many voting members?

- Four hundred thirty-five (435)

The House of Representatives is part of the U.S. Congress. It is considered the lower chamber. The Senate is considered the upper chamber. The members of the House are elected to states based on population. This is why each number of House members per state is different.

22. We elect a U.S. Representative for how many years?

- Two (2)

Representatives are elected for two-year terms. Their reelection is considered on even-numbered years.

23. Name your U.S. Representative.

- Answers will vary. You can find your U.S. Representative here:

  whoismyrepresenative.com

  Some territories may have nonvoting Delegates or Resident Commissioners, or an appropriate answer may be that your territory has no voting Representatives in Congress.

24. Who does a U.S. Senator represent?

- All people of that state

A U.S. Senator represents the people of their state.

25. Why do some states have more Representatives than other states?

- The state's population
- They have more people
- Some states have more people

The number of U.S. Representatives a state has depends on the state's population. For example, the population of California is 39.54 million and it has 53 representatives. Likewise, Alaska has a population of 739,795 and has 1 representative.

26. We elect a President for how many years?

- Four (4)

Presidents have four-year terms. After the four years is up, they are able to be elected for another four years. This makes a total of eight years one person can be president. If a president is elected to office through succession (filling a previous president's incomplete term), the most amount of years they can serve is 10 years, but no more than that.

27. In what month do we vote for President?*

- November

In an election year, presidential elections take place on the first Tuesday after the first Monday in November. Thus, they can take place from November 2 to November 8.

28. What is the name of the President of the United States now?*

- Donald J. Trump
- Donald Trump
- Trump

Donald J. Trump is the full name of the current President of the United States. He was elected to the presidency in the year 2016. His term began January 20, 2017. He is the 45th President of the United States.

29. What is the name of the Vice President of the United States now?

- Michael R. Pence
- Mike Pence
- Pence

Michael R. Pence is the full name of the current Vice President of the United States. Pence was inaugurated as Vice President on January 20, 2017.

30. If the President can no longer serve, who becomes President?

- The Vice President

The Vice President is the first in line to succeed the President were something to happen.

31. If both the President and the Vice President can no longer serve, who becomes President?

- The Speaker of the House

If the President is no longer able to serve, the order of succession is: Vice President, Speaker of the House, Senate president, Secretary of State, and Secretary of Treasury.

32. Who is the Commander in Chief of the military?

- The President

The President is head of the executive office and Commander-in-Chief of the armed forces. This is stated in Article II, Section 2, Clause I of the Constitution.

33. Who signs bills to become laws?

- The President

The bill must pass the Senate and House of Representatives by a majority vote. Then it is sent to the President to sign or veto.

34. Who vetoes bills?

- The President

The President has the ability to veto bills. If the President vetoes a bill, it goes back to Congress. Congress can then move to revote on the issue.

35. What does the President's Cabinet do?

- Advises the President

The President appoints the Cabinet with approval from the Senate to be secretaries for the following departments: State, Defense, Labor, Education, Interior, Agriculture, Transportation, Treasury, Energy, Housing and Urban Development, Commerce, Homeland Security, Health and Human Services, and Veterans Affairs. An additional appointed Cabinet position is the attorney general.

36. What are two Cabinet-level positions?

- Secretary of Agriculture
- Secretary of Commerce
- Secretary of Defense
- Secretary of Education
- Secretary of Energy
- Secretary of Health and Human Services
- Secretary of Homeland Security
- Secretary of Housing and Urban Development
- Secretary of the Interior
- Secretary of Labor
- Secretary of State
- Secretary of Transportation
- Secretary of the Treasury
- Secretary of Veterans Affairs
- Attorney General
- Vice President

The Vice President, attorney general, or heads of the 15 executive departments count as correct answers.

37. What does the judicial branch do?

- Reviews laws
- Explains laws
- Resolves disputes
- Decides if a law goes against the Constitution

The judicial branch interprets the laws and resolves disputes through the court system. The Supreme Court is the highest court. There are five types of courts that are subordinate to the Supreme Court: United States bankruptcy courts, United States Court of Appeals for the Federal Circuit, United States courts of appeals, United States Court of International Trade, and the United States district courts.

38. What is the highest court in the United States?

- The Supreme Court

The Supreme Court was established in 1789. It has authority over all the other courts in the U.S. One power of the Court is judicial review. Judicial review is the ability to invalidate a law for violating the Constitution. On average, the Supreme Court receives 7,000 cases a year. It agrees to hear only around 150 of those cases.

39. How many justices are on the Supreme Court?

- Nine (9)

Supreme Court judges serve life terms. Therefore, they serve until they die, retire, or are impeached and removed from the court.

40. Who is the Chief Justice of the United States now?

- John Roberts (John G. Roberts, Jr.)

The Chief Justice of the Supreme Court is John Roberts, who has served since 2005.

41. Under our Constitution, some powers belong to the federal government. What is one power of the federal government?

- To print money
- To declare war
- To create an army
- To make treaties

The powers given to the federal government are specifically listed in the Constitution under Article I, Section 8. This grants the federal government the power to coin money, regulate commerce, declare war, raise and maintain armed forces, and to establish a Post Office.

42. Under our Constitution, some powers belong to the states. What is one power of the states?

- Provide schooling and education
- Provide protection (police)
- Provide safety (fire departments)
- Give a driver's license
- Approve zoning and land use

Libraries, schools, police departments, driver's license and parking tickets fall under the state and local governments. The Constitution's tenth amendment says that "powers not delegated to the United States by the Constitution . . . are reserved to the States respectively, or to the people."

43. Who is the Governor of your state now?

- Answers will vary

  You can find your Governor here:

  usa.gov/state-governor

  (Note that District of Columbia residents will say that D.C. does not have a Governor).

Governors are the highest-ranking elected officials in the state. Their duties include signing bills into law, serving as commander-in-chief to the state's National Guard, and appointing people to various offices, among others.

44. What is the capital of your state?*

- Answers will vary. (District of Columbia residents should answer that D.C. is not a state and does not have a capital.)

State capitals serve as the center of government for each state.

You can find your state's capital here:

State	Capital
Alabama	Montgomery
Alaska	Juneau
Arizona	Phoenix
Arkansas	Little Rock
California	Sacramento
Colorado	Denver
Connecticut	Hartford
Delaware	Dover

State	Capital
Florida	Tallahassee
Georgia	Atlanta
Hawaii	Honolulu
Idaho	Boise
Illinois	Springfield
Indiana	Indianapolis
Iowa	Des Moines
Kansas	Topeka
Kentucky	Frankfort
Louisiana	Baton Rouge
Maine	Augusta
Maryland	Annapolis
Massachusetts	Boston
Michigan	Lansing
Minnesota	Saint Paul
Mississippi	Jackson
Missouri	Jefferson City
Montana	Helena
Nebraska	Lincoln
Nevada	Carson City
New Hampshire	Concord
New Jersey	Trenton

State	Capital
New Mexico	Santa Fe
New York	Albany
North Carolina	Raleigh
North Dakota	Bismarck
Ohio	Columbus
Oklahoma	Oklahoma City
Oregon	Salem
Pennsylvania	Harrisburg
Rhode Island	Providence
South Carolina	Columbia
South Dakota	Pierre
Tennessee	Nashville
Texas	Austin
Utah	Salt Lake City
Vermont	Montpelier
Virginia	Richmond
Washington	Olympia
West Virginia	Charleston
Wisconsin	Madison
Wyoming	Cheyenne

45. What are the two major political parties in the United States?*

- Democratic and Republican

Either a Democrat or a Republican has won every presidential election since 1852. Either Democrats or Republicans have controlled Congress since at least 1856.

46. What is the political party of the President now?

- Republican (party)

The political party of the current Presidency of Donald Trump is the Republican party.

47. What is the name of the Speaker of the House of Representatives now?

- Nancy P. Pelosi
- Nancy Pelosi
- Pelosi

The Speaker of the House of Representatives is the political and parliamentary leader of the House of Representatives. The Speaker serves as second in line to be president (after the Vice President).

Rights and Responsibilities

48. There are four amendments to the Constitution about who can vote. Describe one of them.

- Citizens eighteen (18) and older can vote.
- You don't have to pay (a poll tax) to vote.
- Any citizen (women and men) can vote.
- A male citizen of any race (can vote).

The 15th amendment says that all American men of all races can vote. The 19th amendment gave women the right to vote. The 24th amendment made poll taxes illegal. The 26th amendment lowered the voting age from 21 to 18.

49. What is one responsibility that is only for United States citizens?*

- Serve on a jury
- Vote in a federal election

Citizens' responsibilities include serving on a jury and voting in a federal election. Taking part in the voting process and in the court system is important in a democratic society.

50. Name one right only for United States citizens.

- Vote in a federal election
- Run for federal office

Citizens' rights ensure that America remains free and prosperous. Rights gives citizens a chance to participate in the democratic process.

51. What are two rights of everyone living in the United States?

- Freedom of expression
- Freedom of speech
- Freedom of assembly
- Freedom to petition the government
- Freedom of religion
- The right to bear arms

Everyone living in the United States is entitled to the above rights which are outlined in the Bill of Rights.

52. What do we show loyalty to when we say the Pledge of Allegiance?

- The United States
- The flag

The Pledge of Allegiance is an oath that expresses allegiance to the flag and to the country.

53. What is one promise you make when you become a United States citizen?

- Give up loyalty to other countries
- Defend the Constitution and laws of the United States
- Obey the laws of the United States
- Serve in the U.S. military (if needed)
- Serve the nation
- Be loyal to the United States

The Oath of Allegiance asks citizens to promise to defend the U.S., give up loyalty to other countries, serve in the military or elsewhere if needed, and to obey U.S. laws.

54. How old do citizens have to be to vote for President?*

- Eighteen (18) and older

Citizens must be eighteen years or older to vote for President. The age was changed from 21 to 18 in 1971 following the Vietnam War.

55. What are two ways that Americans can participate in their democracy?

- Vote
- Join a political party
- Help with a campaign
- Join a civic group
- Join a community group
- Give an elected official your opinion on an issue
- Call Senators and Representatives
- Publicly support or oppose an issue or policy
- Run for office
- Write to a newspaper
- Participating in a democracy

Since the U.S. government is a representative democracy, it is important for citizens to participate in the democratic process. This is so they can have representation. Citizens elect officials. These officials represent citizens' concerns for the country. Part of participating in the democratic process is voting, calling senators and representatives, expressing public opinions, and helping with campaigns.

56. When is the last day you can send in federal income tax forms?*

- April 15

The last day to submit tax returns to the federal government is on April 15 of each year.

57. When must all men register for the Selective Service?

- At age eighteen (18)
- Between eighteen and twenty-six (18 and 26)

The Selected Service is a United States agency that keeps information on those who may be up for a draft. All male U.S. citizens and male immigrant non-citizens must register within 30 days of their 18th birthdays.

American History

Colonial Period and Independence

58. What is one reason colonists came to America?

- Freedom
- Political liberty
- Religious freedom
- Economic opportunity
- Practice their religion
- Escape persecution

European colonists came to America from England, France, Spain, and the Netherlands in the late 16th century. They wanted to escape persecution. They also wanted political and religious freedom.

59. Who lived in America before the Europeans arrived?

- American Indians
- Native Americans

American Indians are indigenous to the United States. Today there are 562 Native American tribes in the

United States. The Cherokee, Sioux, and Navajo are the largest tribes.

60. What group of people was taken to America and sold as slaves?

- Africans
- People from Africa

Slavery in America began in 1619. It ended in 1865 after the Civil War and with the adoption of the 13th amendment.

61. Why did the colonists fight the British?

- Because of high taxes (taxation without representation)
- Because the British army stayed in their houses (boarding, quartering)
- Because they didn't have self-government

The colonists fought the British because they wanted independence from Britain. The colonists felt that King George III and the British army were taking advantage through high taxes and boarding laws. The colonists were not self-governed but wanted freedom from tyranny.

62. Who wrote the Declaration of Independence?

- Thomas Jefferson

The Declaration of Independence was written by Thomas Jefferson in June 1776.

63. When was the Declaration of Independence adopted?

- July 4, 1776

Congress ratified the Declaration of Independence on July 4, 1776. The Declaration of Independence says that the Thirteen Colonies were independent from the rule of Britain.

64. There were 13 original states. Name three.

- New Hampshire
- Massachusetts
- Rhode Island
- Connecticut
- New York
- New Jersey
- Pennsylvania
- Delaware
- Maryland

- Virginia
- North Carolina
- South Carolina
- Georgia

The thirteen colonies were originally British colonies on the North American Atlantic coast. They were founded in the 17th and 18th centuries.

65. What happened at the Constitutional Convention?

- The Constitution was written
- The Founding Fathers wrote the Constitution

The Constitutional Convention took place between 1787 and 1789 in Philadelphia. Its main purpose was to address the issues found in the Articles of Confederation, especially the limitations of a weak central government.

66. When was the Constitution written?

- 1787

The Constitution was written in 1787 during the Constitutional Convention.

67. The Federalist Papers supported the passage of the U.S. Constitution. Name one of the writers.

- James Madison
- Alexander Hamilton
- John Jay
- Publius

The Federalist Papers were written to advocate for the ratification of the Constitution. James Madison, Alexander Hamilton, and John Jay wrote under the pseudonym "Publius."

68. What is one thing Benjamin Franklin is famous for?

- U.S. diplomat
- Oldest member of the Constitutional Convention
- First postmaster General of the United States
- Writer of "Poor Richard's Almanac"
- Started the first free libraries

Benjamin Franklin was a diplomat, statesman, inventor, humorist, civic activist, scientist, politician, political theorist, author, printer, freemason, and postmaster. He is well-known for his discoveries relating to electricity. He also founded civic organizations. Franklin was a delegate at the Constitutional Convention. He signed all four major documents relating to the founding of the United States.

69. Who is the "Father of Our Country"?

- George Washington

George Washington was the first President of the United States. He was also a Founding Father. Washington led American Patriots to victory over Britain.

70. Who was the first President?*

- George Washington

The first presidency of George Washington lasted from 1789 to 1797.

1800s

71. What territory did the United States buy from France in 1803?

- The Louisiana Territory

The buying of this land is known as the Louisiana Purchase. It allowed the U.S. to gain 827,000 square miles of land for $15 million.

72. Name one war fought by the United States in the 1800s.

- War of 1812
- Mexican-American War
- Civil War
- Spanish-American War

A total of four wars were fought by the U.S. in the 1800s. The War of 1812 was between the U.S. and Great Britain. The Mexican-American War was between the U.S. and Mexico. The Civil War was between the American North and South. The Spanish-American War was between the U.S. and Spain.

73. Name the U.S. war between the North and the South.

- The Civil War
- The War between the States

The Civil War was fought from 1861 to 1865 with around 620,000 deaths. The South seceded as the Confederate States of America with Jefferson Davis as the President. Abraham Lincoln was President of the Union.

74. Name one problem that led to the Civil War.

- Slavery
- Economic reasons
- States' rights

The American North and South disagreed over the economics of slavery. They also disagreed on expanding the institution of slavery into new territories in the West. These disagreements brought up the question of states' rights under a central government.

75. What was one important thing that Abraham Lincoln did?*

- Freed the slaves (Emancipation Proclamation)
- Saved (or preserved) the Union
- Led the United States during the Civil War

Abraham Lincoln issued the Emancipation Proclamation on January 1, 1863. This document freed all slaves in the Confederacy. Lincoln was also the Commander-in-Chief during the Civil War. He effectively saved the Union during a time of war.

76. What did the Emancipation Proclamation do?

- Freed the slaves
- Freed slaves in the Confederacy
- Freed slaves in the Confederate states
- Freed slaves in most Southern states

The Emancipation Proclamation was issued in the third year of the Civil War. This document granted slaves freedom within the rebel states.

77. What did Susan B. Anthony do?

- Fought for women's rights
- Fought for civil rights

Susan B. Anthony was an author, speaker, abolitionist, suffragist, and president of the National American Woman Suffrage Association. Anthony illegally voted in the presidential election of 1872. She was arrested and charged with a $100 fine.

Recent American History and Other Important Historical Information

78. Name one war fought by the United States in the 1900s. *

- World War I
- World War II
- Korean War
- Vietnam War
- (Persian) Gulf War

Five wars were fought by the U.S. in the 1900s. The U.S. joined the Allied Powers during World War I in 1917 against Germany, Austria-Hungary, Bulgaria, and the Ottoman Empire (the Central Powers). The United

States joined the Allies during World War II in 1941 and fought Japan, Germany, and Italy (the Axis). The U.S. allied with South Korea in the Korean War from 1950 to 1953, and again they fought with South Vietnam against North Vietnam from 1959 to 1973. The Persian Gulf War lasted from 1990 to 1991 against Iraq as a response to Iraq's invasion of Kuwait.

79. Who was President during World War I?

- Woodrow Wilson

Woodrow Wilson was president from 1913 to 1921. Wilson fought to stay out of the war conflict since it started in 1914. However, he finally asked Congress to declare war in 1917 on the basis of maintaining democracy.

80. Who was the President during the Great Depression and World War II?

- Franklin Roosevelt

Franklin Delano Roosevelt served as president from 1933 to 1945. The Great Depression ended at the time of America's entry into World War II in 1941. Roosevelt was known for expanding the powers of the federal government through the New Deal. The New Deal offered programs and reforms to aid in the Great Depression.

81. Who did the United States fight in World War II?

- Japan, Germany, and Italy

The United States fought Japan, Germany, and Italy during World War II. Japan, Germany, and Italy were known as the Axis powers. The Allies were France, Great Britain, the United States, the Soviet Union, and China.

82. Before he was President, Eisenhower was a general. What war was he in?

- World War II

Eisenhower was Supreme Commander of Allied forces in Western Europe beginning in 1943. He led the invasion of Nazi-occupied Europe in 1944.

83. During the Cold War, what was the main concern of the United States?

- Communism

The Cold War was a state of rivalry between the Soviet Union and the United States after World War II. The Cold War lasted for about 45 years. There was no direct fighting between the United States and the Soviet Union. The United States promised to stop communism while the Soviet Union worked to expand it.

84. What movement tried to end racial discrimination?

- Civil Rights Movement

The Civil Rights Movement took place during the 1950s and 1960s. It was a social justice movement in order for blacks to gain equal rights in the United States.

85. What did Martin Luther King Jr. do?*

- Fought for civil rights
- Worked for equality for all Americans

Martin Luther King Jr. was a Baptist minister and activist. He was the primary spokesperson during the Civil Rights movement. King led nonviolent protests, organized marches, and encouraged civil disobedience. King was assassinated in 1968 in Tennessee.

86. What major event happened on September 11, 2001, in the United States?

- Terrorists attacked the United States

The attacks of 9/11 happened when the Islamic terrorist group, al-Qaeda, hijacked four passenger airliners. The terrorists crashed them into the World Trade Center's North and South towers, the Pentagon, and a field in Pennsylvania.

87. Name one American Indian tribe in the United States.

- Cherokee
- Navajo
- Sioux
- Chippewa
- Choctaw
- Pueblo
- Apache
- Iroquois
- Creek
- Blackfeet
- Seminole

- Cheyenne
- Arawak
- Shawnee
- Mohegan
- Huron
- Oneida
- Lakota
- Crow
- Teton
- Hopi
- Inuit

Since there are many other tribes in the United States, the USCIS Officers will be given a list of federally recognized American Indian tribes.

Integrated Civics

Geography

88. Name one of the two longest rivers in the United States.

- Missouri River
- Mississippi River

The Missouri River is 2,341 miles long and stretches from Western Montana and drains into the Mississippi River in Missouri. The Mississippi River is 2,202 miles long and stretches from Minnesota and drains into the Gulf of Mexico.

89. What ocean is on the West Coast of the United States?

- Pacific Ocean

The Pacific Ocean is on America's western border near California, Oregon, Washington, and Alaska.

90. What ocean is on the East Coast of the United States?

- Atlantic Ocean

The Atlantic Ocean is on America's East Coast. Fourteen states have a shoreline on the Atlantic Ocean.

91. Name one U.S. territory.

- Puerto Rico
- U.S. Virgin Islands
- American Samoa
- Northern Mariana Islands
- Guam

The U.S. currently has sixteen territories, five of which are populated and listed above. The above territories, with the exception of American Samoa, are granted U.S. citizenship at birth.

92. Name one state that borders Canada.

- Maine
- New Hampshire
- Vermont
- New York
- Pennsylvania

- Ohio
- Michigan
- Minnesota
- North Dakota
- Montana
- Idaho
- Washington
- Alaska

Thirteen U.S. states border Canada in the northern United States.

93. Name one state that borders Mexico.

- California
- Arizona
- New Mexico
- Texas

The states that border Mexico are California, Arizona, New Mexico, and Texas. This area stretches for 1,954 miles.

94. What is the capital of the United States?*

- Washington, D.C.

Washington D.C. became the capital of the United States in 1790 when the Residence Act was signed. The District is not part of any state. It was made to serve as a federal district under the authority of Congress.

95. Where is the Statue of Liberty?*

- New York (Harbor)
- Liberty Island
- (Additionally, you can say New Jersey, near New York City, and on the Hudson River.)

The Statue of Liberty was a gift to the United States from France. It is meant to honor the friendship between the two countries. The statue is a robed Roman liberty goddess named Libertas. She holds a message on her tablet that says July 4, 1776 (Independence Day) in roman numerals.

Symbols

96. Why does the flag have 13 stripes?

- Because there were 13 original colonies
- Because the stripes represent the original colonies

The flag has 13 stripes. They symbolize the 13 colonies that declared their independence from Great Britain.

97. Why does the flag have 50 stars?*

- Because there is one star for each state
- Because each star represents a state
- Because there are 50 states

The stars on the American flag stand for the 50 states. A star was added each time the U.S. took on a state. Hawaii was the last state added in 1959.

98. What is the name of the national anthem?

- The Star-Spangled Banner

Francis Scott Key wrote the Star-Spangled Banner in 1814. He wrote it after the Battle of Baltimore during the War of 1812.

Holidays

99. When do we celebrate Independence Day?*

- July 4

July 4 is the day the Declaration of Independence was published in 1776.

100. Name two national holidays.

- New Year's Day
- Martin Luther King, Jr. Day
- Presidents' Day
- Memorial Day
- Independence Day
- Labor Day
- Columbus Day
- Veterans Day
- Thanksgiving
- Christmas

National holidays are recognized by the U.S. government. Federal employees are paid on national holidays. Also, non-essential federal government offices are closed.

Test Yourself

1. What is the supreme law of the land?

2. What does the Constitution do?

3. The idea of self-government is in the first three words of the Constitution. What are these words?

4. What is an amendment?

5. What do we call the first ten amendments to the Constitution?

6. What is one right or freedom from the First Amendment?*

7. How many amendments does the Constitution have?

8. What did the Declaration of Independence do?

9. What are two rights in the Declaration of Independence?

10. What is freedom of religion?

11. What is the economic system in the United States?*

12. What is the "rule of law"?

13. Name one branch or part of the government.*

14. What stops one branch of government from becoming too powerful?

15. Who is in charge of the executive branch?

16. Who makes federal laws?

17. What are the two parts of the U.S. Congress?*

18. How many U.S. Senators are there?

19. We elect a U.S. Senator for how many years?

20. Who is one of your state's U.S. Senators now?*

21. The House of Representatives has how many voting members?

22. We elect a U.S. Representative for how many years?

23. Name your U.S. Representative.

24. Who does a U.S. Senator represent?

25. Why do some states have more Representatives than other states?

26. We elect a President for how many years?

27. In what month do we vote for President?*

28. What is the name of the President of the United States now?*

29. What is the name of the Vice President of the United States now?

30. If the President can no longer serve, who becomes President?

31. If both the President and the Vice President can no longer serve, who becomes President?

32. Who is the Commander in Chief of the military?

33. Who signs bills to become laws?

34. Who vetoes bills?

35. What does the President's Cabinet do?

36. What are two Cabinet-level positions?

37. What does the judicial branch do?

38. What is the highest court in the United States?

39. How many justices are on the Supreme Court?

40. Who is the Chief Justice of the United States now?

41. Under our Constitution, some powers belong to the federal government. What is one power of the federal government?

42. Under our Constitution, some powers belong to the states. What is one power of the states?

43. Who is the Governor of your state now?

44. What is the capital of your state?*

45. What are the two major political parties in the United States?*

46. What is the political party of the President now?

47. What is the name of the Speaker of the House of Representatives now?

48. There are four amendments to the Constitution about who can vote. Describe one of them.

49. What is one responsibility that is only for United States citizens?*

50. Name one right only for United States citizens.

51. What are two rights of everyone living in the United States?

52. What do we show loyalty to when we say the Pledge of Allegiance?

53. What is one promise you make when you become a United States citizen?

54. How old do citizens have to be to vote for President?*

55. What are two ways that Americans can participate in their democracy?

56. When is the last day you can send in federal income tax forms?*

57. When must all men register for the Selective Service?

58. What is one reason colonists came to America?

59. Who lived in America before the Europeans arrived?

60. What group of people was taken to America and sold as slaves?

61. Why did the colonists fight the British?

62. Who wrote the Declaration of Independence?

63. When was the Declaration of Independence adopted?

64. There were 13 original states. Name three.

65. What happened at the Constitutional Convention?

66. When was the Constitution written?

67. The Federalist Papers supported the passage of the U.S. Constitution. Name one of the writers.

68. What is one thing Benjamin Franklin is famous for?

69. Who is the "Father of Our Country"?

70. Who was the first President?*

71. What territory did the United States buy from France in 1803?

72. Name one war fought by the United States in the 1800s.

73. Name the U.S. war between the North and the South.

74. Name one problem that led to the Civil War.

75. What was one important thing that Abraham Lincoln did?*

76. What did the Emancipation Proclamation do?

77. What did Susan B. Anthony do?

78. Name one war fought by the United States in the 1900s. *

79. Who was President during World War I?

80. Who was the President during the Great Depression and World War II?

81. Who did the United States fight in World War II?

82. Before he was President, Eisenhower was a general. What war was he in?

83. During the Cold War, what was the main concern of the United States?

84. What movement tried to end racial discrimination?

85. What did Martin Luther King Jr. do?*

86. What major event happened on September 11, 2001, in the United States?

87. Name one American Indian tribe in the United States.

88. Name one of the two longest rivers in the United States.

89. What ocean is on the West Coast of the United States?

90. What ocean is on the East Coast of the United States?

91. Name one U.S. territory.

92. Name one state that borders Canada.

93. Name one state that borders Mexico.

94. What is the capital of the United States?*

95. Where is the Statue of Liberty?*

96. Why does the flag have 13 stripes?

97. Why does the flag have 50 stars?*

98. What is the name of the national anthem?

99. When do we celebrate Independence Day?*

100. Name two national holidays.

Greetings!

First, we would like to give a huge "thank you" for choosing us and this study guide for your naturalization process. We hope that it will lead you to success in the process and for years to come.

We strive for excellence in our products, and if you have any comments or concerns over the quality of something in this study guide, please send us an email so that we can improve.

We are continually producing and updating study guides in several different subjects. If you are looking for something in particular, all of our products are available on Amazon. You may also send us an email!

Sincerely,
APEX Test Prep
info@apexprep.com

Made in the USA
Coppell, TX
08 November 2020

41005539R00046